A New True Book

EXPERIMENTS WITH MAGNETS

By Helen J. Challand

CHILDRENS PRESS ®

CHICAGO

Young scientists study a
magnet's energy field.

PHOTO CREDITS

Tony Freeman Photographs—2, 4 (left), 6
(2 photos), 7 (left), 10, 11 (left), 13 (right), 14, 23
(2 photos), 24, 26 (2 photos), 28 (2 photos), 30
(2 photos), 31, 32, 34, 36, 37, 39

Jet Propulsion Laboratory—45

Journalism Services: © Joseph Jacobson—4
(right)

NASA—44

Nawrocki Stock Photo: © Jim Wright—Cover, 7
(right), 15, 16, 17, 19, 21

Root Resources: © Mary Root—20

© Jerome Wyckoff—13 (left)

John Forsberg—9, 11 (right), 18, 41, 42

Library of Congress Cataloging-in-Publication Data

Challand, Helen J.
  Experiments with magnets.

  (A New true book)
  Includes index.
  Summary: Suggests experiments introducing magnets
and magnetism, demonstrating the magnetic field and
the properties, strength, and uses of magnets.
  1. Magnets—Experiments—Juvenile literature.
[1. Magnets—Experiments.   2. Magnetism—Experiments.
3. Experiments]   I. Title.
QC757.5.C47   1986   538'.2   85-30851
ISBN 0-516-01279-7

TABLE OF CONTENTS

Giant cranes with electromagnets are used to move heavy pieces of metal.

USEFUL MAGNETS

People use magnets every day in their business, at home, or for recreation.

Cranes with huge magnets are used in junkyards to move wrecked cars and other objects around.

Police use large magnets on the end of ropes to search the bottom of lakes

A magnet holds the lid (left). Magnets also can hold notes onto the door of a refrigerator (above).

for guns and other objects related to a crime.

An electric can opener has a magnet to hold the lid as it is being cut off.

The refrigerator door stays closed because of magnets.

Door bell (left) and
two compasses (above)

A door bell, telephone, and television set would not work without magnets.

How could we explore without a compass? Christopher Columbus used one when he discovered North America. Magnetism is indeed a very important form of energy.

WHAT IS A MAGNET?

A magnet is an object that can push or pick up some things. These materials must be made of iron, steel, nickel, or cobalt. A magnet must also be made of these materials.

All things are made of tiny bits or atoms. In things that are not magnetized the atoms are disorganized. If we could see inside an ordinary iron

nail the atoms would be
going in all directions.
Study this drawing.

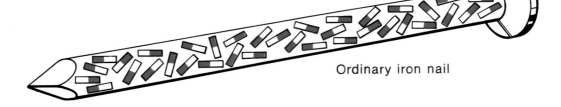

Ordinary iron nail

This iron nail can be
turned into a magnet. By
using a force or energy all
the atoms can be lined up
in one direction. The nail
is now magnetized.

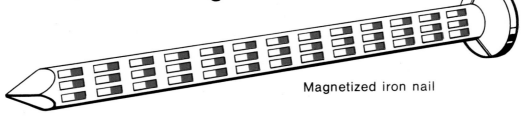

Magnetized iron nail

A hanging magnet will point to the different poles.

The force, the push or pull, of a magnet is strongest at its ends. These ends are called poles. When a magnet is hanging freely on the end of a string, one end will point to the earth's North Pole. The other end will point to the South Pole. Atoms also have north and

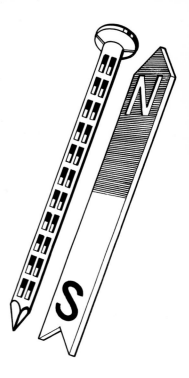

Young scientist uses a
magnet to pull iron nails.

south poles. In a
magnetized nail the atoms
would line up, too.

Now you can see the
force that can pull if all
the poles of one kind are
facing in one direction.

SEEING
A MAGNETIC FIELD

The space around a magnet is called a magnetic field. It is the area where the force of a magnet acts or can be felt. Iron filings can be used to see these lines of force.

Sprinkle iron filings on magnets of different shapes. If you don't have

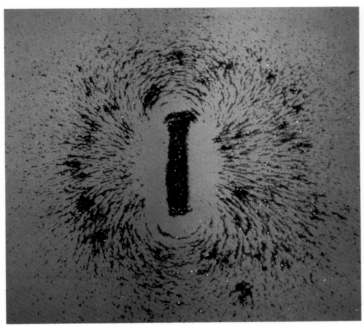

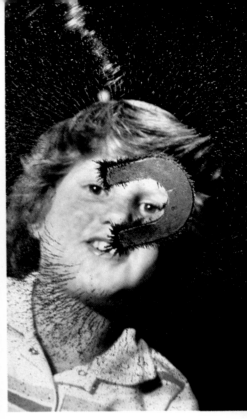

Magnetic field of a bar
magnet (left) and a
horseshoe magnet (above).

filings, cut steel wool into
tiny bits. Place a clear
sheet of plastic on top of
the magnet. This makes it
easier to return the iron
filings to their container.

Opposite magnetic poles attract each other.

PUSH OR PULL

The north pole of a magnet pulls or attracts the south pole of a magnet. One can feel this force. Bring the north pole of one magnet close to the south pole of a second magnet. What happens?

Pattern of iron filings
shows the attraction
between two bar magnets.

One can also see the
lines of force when
opposite poles are near
each other. Place two
magnets with the opposite
poles one inch apart.
Sprinkle iron filings over
both magnets. What is the
pattern of the filings?

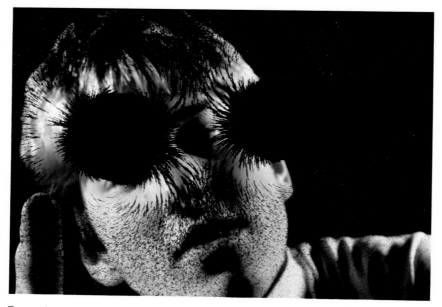
Round magnets with north poles at opposite ends.

One can experiment and see the force of the magnetic field. Use rolling or round magnets for this experiment.

Lay two magnets close to each other with the opposite poles facing each other. What happens?

Now position the rolling magnets with the same or like poles facing each other. Sprinkle iron filings over both. What design do they make now? Can you see the lines of force pushing or repelling?

Round magnets with the same poles facing each other

Not only can magnets push and pull, but they also can lift. This lifting force can be seen by setting up a holding frame. Glue pencils or dowels to a wooden base. Follow the pattern in the drawing. The sticks should be placed just far enough apart to

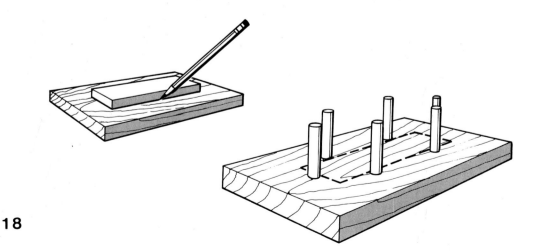

hold the magnets. Place
one magnet on top of the
other magnet between the
sticks. Be sure the north
or like poles are at the
same end. What happens
to the top magnet?

Close-up of
magnetite

NATURAL MAGNETS

There are some rocks in
the ground that are
magnets. They are made
of an iron ore called
magnetite. Years ago
people called them magic

stones. A natural magnet is called a lodestone. This means leading stone. When brought near iron things it will grab them. Lodestones have north and south poles just as do artificial magnets. Some even have several sets of poles.

Paper clip held by a lodestone

TEMPORARY MAGNETS

A piece of iron or steel can be made to act as a magnet for a short time. Then it loses its magnetism. It is called a temporary magnet.

An iron nail, darning needle, or long sewing needle can be used to make a temporary magnet. Take a permanent or artificial magnet and stroke the nail or needle in one direction. Do this fifty to a hundred times. The pull of the permanent magnet will slowly line up the atoms in the nail or needle. It becomes magnetized. Test this temporary magnet by picking up one paper clip.

A temporary magnet (right) can be made by stroking a nail (left) with a magnet.

Temporary magnet
holding paper clips

Take a second paper clip
and touch it to the first
one. Be careful that it
does not touch the
magnet. Is the first paper
clip also magnetized? How
long does the nail hang on
to the clips? That is the
reason it is called a
temporary magnet.

HOW STRONG
IS A MAGNET ?

The strength of each
kind of magnet can be
tested. Select a number of
permanent magnets of
different shapes and sizes.
Use a pile of thumbtacks
or pins for this experiment.
Use only one pole of the
magnet to pick up as
many objects from the pile
as will hold to the magnet.
Count the number of pins

Young scientists experiment in order to
find out the strength of their magnets.

or tacks attached to the
pole. Do this for each
magnet. Does the size or
shape affect the amount of
pull the magnet has?

26

GRAB BAG

Collect a lot of objects
for this game: glass
marble, penny, dime,
nickel, silver spoon, gold
pin, iron nail, pin, needle,
thumbtack, plastic, cork,
wood, brass screw,
aluminum nail, cloth, rubber
eraser, lead in a pencil,
and many other materials.
Sort them into two piles.
One pile is for all things
that you think a magnet

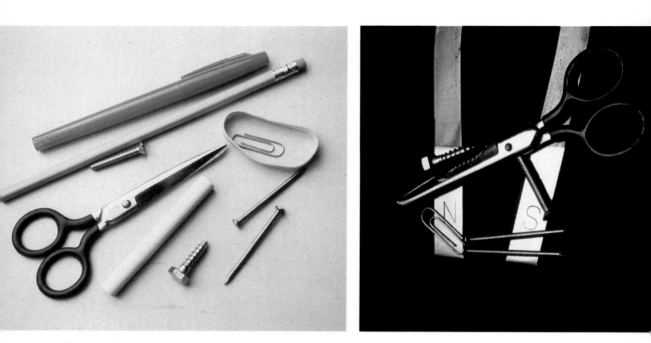

Some of these objects will not be attracted to a magnet.

will pick up. The other is things that will not be attracted to a magnet. Now test your predictions or guesses by using a magnet. How good a scientist were you?

TRY TO STOP MAGNETISM

The force a magnet has is in the area around it. What if you put something besides air between the magnet and something it will pick up? Will the magnet still work? Let's see.

Tie a paper clip to one end of a piece of string. Tape the other end of the string to the table. Bring the magnet close enough

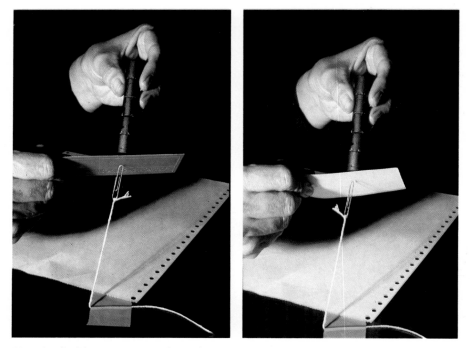

Plastic (left) and paper (right) let magnetism go through.

to the clip to hold it in the air. Do not let the magnet touch the paper clip. Now hold thin sheets of different materials between the magnet and clip. Use paper, cardboard, cork,

glass, wood, plastic, and
metal. If the paper clip
falls to the table, you know
that material will not let
magnetism go through it.

Drop a paper clip into a
bowl of water. Bring a
magnet close to the clip.
Does the force of
magnetism go through
water?

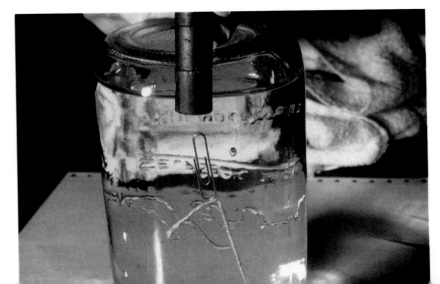

ELECTROMAGNET

A current of electricity
can produce magnetism.
These things are needed

An electromagnet
can be made with
a nail and a battery

to produce a magnet: a
dry cell or battery,
insulated or bell wire, and
a large iron nail. The wire
should be wrapped around
the nail a number of times.
The insulation must be
taken off the last inch of
the two wire ends. Wind
one end of the wire
around one battery terminal
and wind the other wire
around the other terminal.

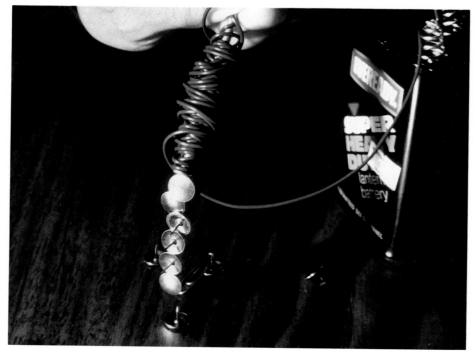

An electromagnet holding tacks

The current in the battery
is now flowing through the
wire. This causes a
magnetic field around the
nail. It is a magnet with a
north and south pole. Use
the magnet to pick up a

number of tacks. Remove
one wire from one
terminal. What happens to
the tacks? An
electromagnet works only
when electricity is present.
It is a temporary magnet.

The poles of an
electromagnet can be
reversed. A compass can
be used to check this out.
Place the compass near
the nail. Hook the wire to
the battery terminals.

In a compass the magnetic needle will point to the magnetic north. What happens to the needle after you switch the wires on the electromagnet?

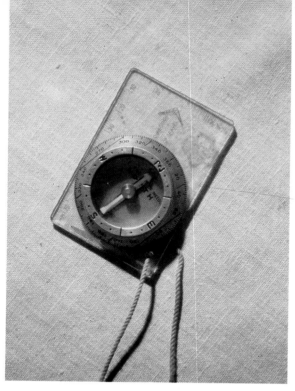

Remember which way the compass is pointing. Switch the wires on the dry cell from one terminal to the other. What happens to the way the compass is pointing? It is now pointing in the opposite direction.

Adding wire increases the power of this electromagnet

An electromagnet can be made stronger. Double the number of turns of wire on the nail. How many tacks will it pick up now? Use two dry cells instead of one. The electromagnet should be twice as strong.

BE CAREFUL

Permanent magnets must be handled with care if they are to keep their energy. Dropping a magnet will jar the molecules out of line. Extreme heat will also upset the magnetic field of a magnet. Always store magnets with the north pole of one next to the south pole of another.

Good magnets come with keepers. A keeper is

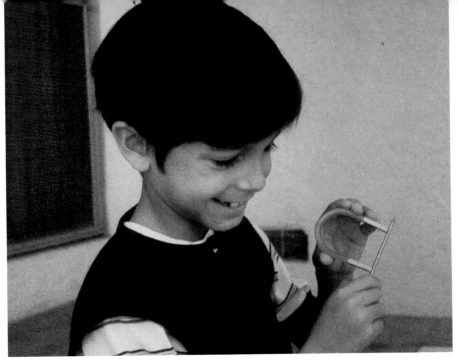

A keeper bar protects this horseshoe magnet.

a piece of iron that is placed across the opposite poles. It is especially important with U-shaped and horseshoe magnets. If you don't have a keeper, a nail or other soft piece of iron will work.

THE BIGGEST MAGNET OF ALL

Did you know that our planet earth is a huge magnet? Inside the earth, the center or inner core is probably solid. We think it is made of iron and nickel. The outer core is more like a thick pudding. The moving of the inner core inside the outer core makes a magnetic field.

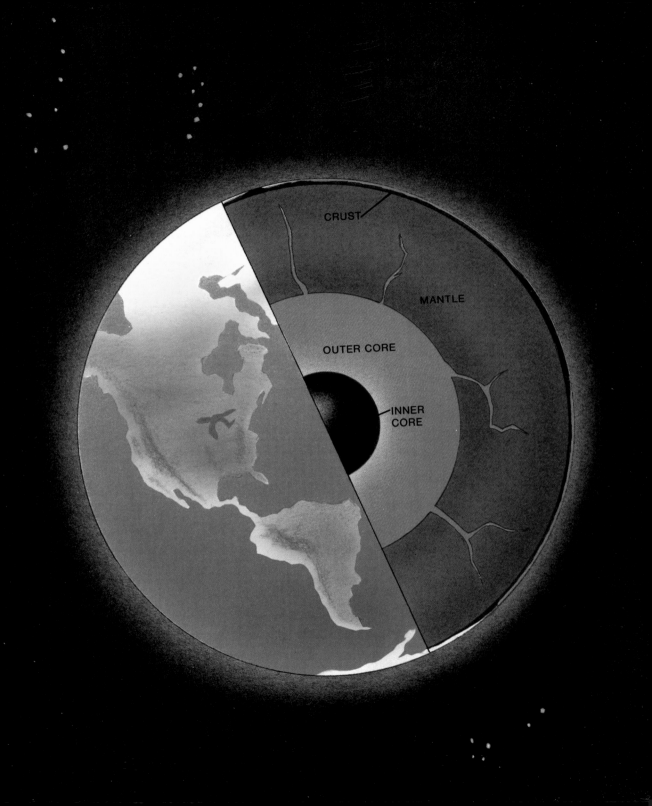

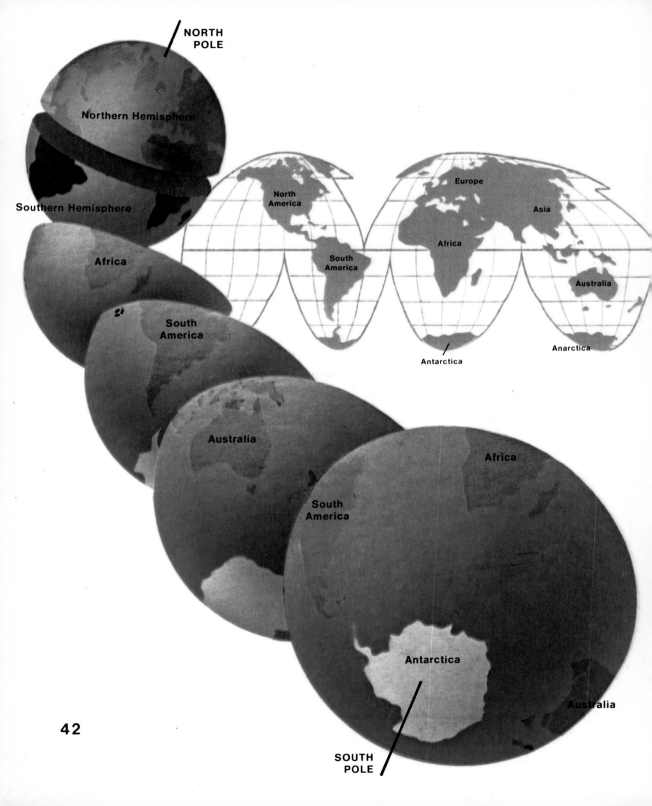

NORTH POLE

Northern Hemisphere

Southern Hemisphere

Africa

South America

Australia

South America

Australia

Africa

Antarctica

Australia

SOUTH POLE

North America

South America

Europe

Asia

Africa

Australia

Antarctica

Anarctica

42

This is why the earth has a North Pole in the Arctic Circle and a South Pole in the Antarctic Circle. If the earth had no magnetic poles, then a free-hanging magnet would not line up pointing to the north and south. The earth's magnetism is much weaker than a good magnet. Our earth isn't really the

All planets have magnetism.

biggest magnet. Scientists
believe that all the planets,
the sun, and other stars
have magnetism. The
whole universe has this
invisible force. Scientists

Artist's painting of Voyager II exploring Uranus in 1986 (above).
Voyager II will explore Neptune in 1989.

are using satellites and
other space probes to
learn more about magnetic
fields beyond the earth.

WORDS YOU SHOULD KNOW

atom(AT • um) — the smallest part of anything that can exist alone

attract(uh • TRACT) — to pull something toward itself

electromagnet(ih • lek • troh • MAG • net) — a temporary magnet that has a magnetic force only when electric current is passed through it

energy(EN • er • jee) — the power to do work

keeper(KEE • purr) — a piece of iron placed across the poles of a permanent magnet when it is stored or not in use, in order to keep the magnet's energy from being lost

lodestone(LOHD • stohn) — a natural magnet, made of an iron ore called magnetite

magnetic field(mag • NET • ik FEELD) — the space around a magnet in which the magnetic force can be felt or seen to exist

molecule(MAHL • ih • kyool) — the smallest part of something, made of one or more atoms

poles(POHLZ) — the two regions at the ends of a magnet (the north pole and south pole) where magnetic force is strongest

repel(rih • PELL) — to push or force away

INDEX

About the author

Helen J. Challand earned her M.A. and Ph.D. from Northwestern University. She currently is Chair of the Science Department at National College of Education and Coordinator of Undergraduate Studies for the college's West Suburban Campus.

An experienced classroom teacher and science consultant, Dr. Challand has worked on science projects for Scott Foresman and Company, Rand McNally Publishers, Harper-Row Publishers, Encyclopedia Britannica Films, Coronet Films, and Journal Films. She is the author of Earthquakes, Plants Without Seeds, Volcanoes, Experiments with Electricity, *and* Experiments with Magnets *in the True Book series and served as associate editor for the* Young People's Science Encyclopedia *published by Childrens Press.*